Priesthood Today

Lessons from the Curé d'Ars

by
Patrick O'Donoghue
emeritus Bishop of Lancaster

*All booklets are published thanks to the
generous support of the members of the
Catholic Truth Society*

CATHOLIC TRUTH SOCIETY
PUBLISHERS TO THE HOLY SEE

Contents

Preface

This booklet is based on talks I gave to priests of the Diocese of Northampton during their retreat in Ars in May 2009. Held during the week after my retirement as the Bishop of Lancaster, it was a delight to spend time with my brother priests reflecting on the nature of the priesthood in the light of the ministry of the *Curé d'Ars*. I am convinced that one hundred and fifty years after Jean Vianney's death, the charisms of this remarkable priest's life still have the power to inspire and transform our own ministry.

After serving the People of God for almost sixteen years as a bishop in Westminster and Lancaster I have returned to Cork to serve as an assistant priest in the parish of Bantry. I can think of nothing better than to spend the rest of my days as a pastor living close to the people, sharing Christ through the Word of God and the sacraments.

As you may know, during my last years as the Bishop of Lancaster my diocese undertook the *Fit for Mission?* review, that examined all aspects of the sacramental and mission life of the diocese. It provided us with a snap shot of the health of our Christian discipleship in the three dimensions of our lives - family, parish and school - and provided recommendations for strengthening our Catholic identity. I am convinced that we will only begin to challenge the widespread dissent, disloyalty and disobedience that is harming the Church through the leadership and example of *holy* priests.

Pope Benedict XVI has called a special Year for Priests principally to encourage priests, diocesan and religious, to pursue the perfection of Christ, which he describes as, *'that indispensable struggle for moral perfection which must dwell in every truly priestly heart.'*

If our people are to embrace the discipline and commitment necessary to become a holy people, we priests must re-engage with renewed passion and commitment in this 'indispensable struggle for moral perfection'. I hope this booklet contributes to this most important challenge of our day, that we all become, through our co-operation with grace, more and more like Our Lord, Jesus Christ. Can there be anything more important or more joyful than this?

I would like to thank Peter Doyle, Bishop of Northampton, for giving me the opportunity to share my thoughts on the priesthood with his priests.

Patrick O'Donoghue
Emeritus Bishop of Lancaster

A priest's courage to proclaim Salvation

The theme of these reflections is 'Rich in Christ, rich in love', and it invites us to consider the identity, role, spirituality and formation of the priest.

Recently the Holy Father announced a Year for Priests, (from 16th June 2009 to June 2010) following the theme, 'Faithfulness of Christ, faithfulness of priests'. Pope Benedict has given an indication of how we, as priests, should approach this special year of reflection and formation, which we would do well to consider.

How do we distinguish between the baptismal and ministerial priesthood? In what ways has this distinction become confused? What does it mean to say that the priest is sacramentally configured to Christ the Head? How is this lived out in day to day life? Pope Benedict said, 'Without the ministry of priests, there would be no Eucharist, no mission, not even the Church'. Do we believe this? What responsibilities does this give us as priests? (*Letter Proclaiming a Year for Priests on the 150th anniversary of the 'Dies Natalis' of the Curé of Ars*).

Pope Benedict emphasises the importance of discipline to the 'hierarchical' and 'doctrinal' dimensions of the Church - what is the nature of this discipline? Why has discipline become such a problem for priests and people?

Pope Benedict states that the 'indispensable struggle for moral perfection' must truly dwell in the heart of every priest. Do we still believe that sanctity is a possibility, or are we only human? Do we still believe that Jesus, the incarnate Son of God, is the answer to our deepest desires for happiness, and the desires of all human hearts?

Bishop Patrick Casey ordained me priest back in my home parish of Mourne Abbey, Cork, in 1967, and now 42 years later it gives me great joy to reflect on what it means to be a priest in the 21st century in a world that is very different to the world I first served as a young priest.

What does 'crisis' mean?

Pope Benedict, when he was Cardinal Ratzinger, once said 'the crisis of the Church today is before all else a crisis of priests.' (*The Ratzinger Report*).

Personally, I do not adopt a 'doom and gloom' perspective about the future of the Church and the priesthood because I genuinely have hope that the Holy Spirit turns all things to the good. However I do agree with Cardinal Ratzinger that we are facing a crisis in the Church, and at the heart of this crisis is a crisis among priests, and a crisis about priests among many of the laity.

We hear the word 'crisis' a lot nowadays, the ecology crisis, the world financial crisis, the crisis facing the Church. But what does *crisis* mean? It comes from the Greek word, meaning decision, time of decision. Instead of being a word we dread, a word that leaves us feeling powerless, the word *crisis* confronts us with the truth of the situation - we are faced with a decision, a choice of how to respond, how to act.

I think it is important that priests take the opportunity to frankly and honestly confront the challenges that face us, and even come to decisions about what needs to be done personally and as a body of priests.

Light and dark after Vatican II

A good starting point would be to consider both the positive and negative things that have faced the priesthood since the Second Vatican Council. The positive developments for the priesthood since Vatican II could be listed as follows:

Much reduced clericalism

The re-emergence of the *People of God and Body of Christ* models of the Church, and the development of the theology and role of the laity, has resulted in a diversity of vocations and charisms in the Church. One of the results of this is that, thankfully, priests are no longer an isolated, autonomous caste in the Church they serve.

True collaborative ministry

When the distinct roles and responsibilities of the clergy and laity are recognised and respected, true and fruitful collaboration in service of the sacramental and mission life of the Church occurs. 'Collaborative ministry' only becomes a 'dirty' word when it is either used as a cover for anticlericalism and a hi-jacking of the priest's role by others with a will-to-power, or a diminishment of the laity to just being 'Father's helpers'.

A growing spirit of fraternity

Since Vatican II greater efforts have been taken to create a spirit of fraternity between bishop and priests, and between priests. As it says in the *Decree on Bishops*, 'A bishop should always welcome priests with a special love...He should regard his priests as sons and friends...his readiness to listen to them and by his trusting familiarity' (*Christus Dominus*, 16).

Richer sacramental life

The development of the Church's sacramental theology has led to a growing understanding of the sacraments as our participation in the 'mysteries of Christ' rather than as the means of being 'zapped' by grace. This, in turn, has made the liturgy of the Word much more important in the rite of all the sacraments. Altogether this has enriched the priests' celebration of the sacraments.

Biblical spirituality

Since Vatican II, in particular *Dei Verbum*, sacred Scripture has become fundamental to the spirituality of many priests, through *Lectio* or other forms of meditation. This has had a positive influence on homiletics and catechesis, in some cases.

Friendship

Where once before 'particular friendships' were viewed with suspicion and apprehension, now it is universally accepted that friendship, with both sexes, is essential for the happiness and well-being of priests. This experience of love has enriched and matured the lives of so many priests. Also, friendships with other Christians has gone from being a source of scandal or threat to something welcomed as a fruit of ecumenism.

On the other hand, there are what can be considered negative developments for the priesthood since Vatican II, and they could include the following:

Loss of brother priests

The staggering and heart-breaking loss of priests in the aftermath of Vatican II has left painful wounds in the Church, including grief and a loss of confidence among many of that generation who remain. Also, the decline in the number of new priests being ordained has a disheartening and discouraging effect.

Dissent and disobedience

We are living in an unprecedented period in the life of the Church when countless individual priests, and laity, even bishops, believe they are free to decide what it means to be Catholic for themselves. For example, we have witnessed a wholesale rejection of the Church's perennial teaching against contraception. This is the litmus test of the acceptance of obedience in the Church. How many priests support *Gaudium et Spes'* crystal clear rejection of contraception, upheld by successive Popes - Paul VI, John Paul II, Benedict XVI? If we reject their teaching on this matter we are saying, as priests, that we know better than the successor to Peter! Is this tenable in a priest?

Disloyalty

This is related to dissent and disobedience but is to do with the relationship between priest and bishop, and bishop and Pope. It is not uncommon for cliques to grow up among priests against the current bishop that ignore, with disdain, his directives and advice. Sometimes it seems that some parish priests and parishes declare UDI (Unilateral Declaration of Independence) from the bishop and the diocese.

There is also danger of this developing in a group of bishops in their attitude to the reigning Pope. The idea that there could be theological differences between a bishop and the Pope is just an incredible thing to admit, but it is the truth. I suppose if priests see bishops showing disloyalty to the Pope it is hardly surprising that they, in turn, show disloyalty to their bishop. We all know what Jesus said about a divided house.

Conspiracy of silence

This cocktail of dissent, disobedience and disloyalty has resulted in what I call a 'conspiracy of silence' amongst groups in the Church. There is no real dialogue or willingness to talk openly and honestly about our differences. For example, I don't know why my *Fit for Mission?* documents met a wall of silence among the bishops in this country. All I did was re-iterate the teaching of the Church, but this has been treated as unacceptable and unspeakable. Why?

Secularisation

Last year Pope Benedict warned us to be on our guard against the secularisation of the Church. By this he meant that priests and people were accepting consumerism and hedonism as a way of life. Can we truly say that our lives are known as examples of 'sacrifice' and 'service'? It seems to me that we, too, have accepted the type of pop-psychology that dismisses 'self-denial' and self-sacrifice as harmful and 'sado-masochistic'.

Anti-intellectualism

One of the most surprising things to hear is that it's a waste of time to write, say, a 130-page document on the Church, because the priests will not read it. It is even possible to hear, in the Church of St Augustine and St Thomas Aquinas, priests use the words 'theology' and 'theologian' as pejoratives! Often 'pastoral experience' is held up against 'theology' as if they were mutually exclusive. In my opinion, this is deeply unhealthy and harmful to the Church. There is much good, sound, faithful theology being undertaken at present that will enrich the Church if, and only if, the priests start engaging with it.

Sex abuse scandals

Don't all our hearts sink when we hear those words! How much unspeakable harm has been done to children by these predatory paedophiles, who are also our brother priests? The harm they have done to the spreading of the Gospel and the mission of the Church is incalculable. Our understanding of the nature of this crime has developed after these past two decades, and hopefully children are better protected, but we have to live with the consequences of suspicion and distrust, which for the majority of us is undeserved and so very hurtful. This is the reality of Sin.

Liturgism

By this I mean the tendency among some clergy and laity to solely focus on the liturgy and sacramental life, ignoring our mission to go out of the church building into the world where suffering humanity lives! For a century the Church has been saying that social justice should be a concern of Catholics equal to attending Mass on Sunday. How many believe this? How many priests encourage this?

Despite all this I remain a man of hope! By disposition and experience I seek to see the positive, the rumour of grace in situations no matter how bad it first appears. I am not a prophet of doom, and in my *Fit for Mission?* documents I have *not* sought to be a Jeremiah announcing the impending destruction of the Church in this country!

All in all, we have much to be grateful for as a result of the Second Vatican Council, which was truly a marvellous work of the Holy Spirit.

The tyranny of the autonomous conscience

But as well as being a man of hope, I am also a realist who strongly believes that we have to speak the truth about the health of the Church in this country. I do not believe that I am exaggerating when I say that the Catholic Church in this country and in the West is in danger of splitting into factions openly at war with each other. The simple fact is that for the first time in the history of the Church we have a significant number of practicing Catholics - both liberals and traditionalists - who believe that they can decide what it means to be Catholic. We have priests, deacons, religious, laity and even some bishops who believe they have the right to decide what doctrines and morals to affirm or ignore.

As I've said elsewhere, many Catholics hold that if - in conscience - they disagree with any teaching of the Church then they have the freedom - even the duty - to reject that teaching. For many, the authority of the autonomous conscience has overthrown the authority of Christ given to Peter and the Apostles. In some circles, the infallibility of the Pope has been replaced by the infallibility of individual conscience.

So on the liberal side, we have Catholics assuming in their day-to-day lives that their opinions about doctrine and morals are right, and the Pope and the Church's 2,000 years reflection on God's revelation is wrong about so many things, like contraception, IVF, homosexuality, the divinity of Jesus, the importance of devotion to Mary, and the Saints, the necessity of regular confession, the importance of 'objective' morality, and much more.

On the so called 'traditionalist' side, we have Catholics assuming in their day-to-day lives that their opinions about the teachings of the Second Vatican Council are right and a succession of Popes, Bishops, and priests are wrong about liturgy, the importance of ecumenism, the obligation of involvement in justice and peace, the development of lay theology and ministry, the role of women in the Church, and much more.

The misuse of freedom

As Pope Benedict so frankly and painfully wrote in his letter to bishops following the removal of excommunication on the four bishops consecrated by Archbishop Lefebvre:

'I was surprised at the directness with which that passage speaks to us about the present moment: "Do not use your freedom as an opportunity for the flesh, but through love be servants of one another. For the whole law is fulfilled in one word: 'You shall love your neighbour as yourself'. But if you bite and devour one another, take heed that you are not consumed by one another." (*Ga* 5:13-15)... sad to say, this "biting and devouring" also exists in the Church today, as expression of a poorly understood freedom. Should we be surprised that we too are no better than the Galatians? That at the very least we are threatened by the same temptations? That we must always learn anew the proper use of freedom? And that we must always learn anew the supreme priority, which is love?'

The Holy Father is right to warn us about the dangers of the misuse of freedom within the Church, and the threat this poses to the future of the Church. I do not think it is a co-incidence that in the same week that he released his unprecedented letter about the threats to the Church, he also announced the special year for priests. It is only through the leadership, spirituality and service of priests, working in collaboration with the successor of Peter and those bishops in communion with him, that we will be able to bring healing and direction to our fragmenting Church.

The challenge of St John Vianney

As the climax of the Year for Priests, Pope Benedict has also revealed his intention to proclaim St Jean Marie

Vianney as patron saint of all the priests of the world, as we commemorate the 150th anniversary of the Curé d'Ars' death. As you know, at present St Jean Vianney is patron saint of parish priests. I once had the good fortune of being able to accompany the younger priests of Lancaster diocese for a week's retreat in Ars. I can think of no more fitting way to mark the end of my active ministry as a diocesan bishop than to have spent time praying before the tomb of this great 'priest of priests'.

Even though I have a devotion to St Jean Vianney, I can't help asking these questions: Why are we drawn to this man who was a parish priest in an obscure French village 150 years ago? Why is the Holy Father holding him up as a model for priests throughout the world who face challenges the *Curé d'Ars* would never have dreamed of? How can this priest of an 19th century French village help us be priests today? We've had great theologian priests, like Fr Karl Rahner, Fr Hans urs Von Balthasar and Fr Henri de Lubac. We've had great martyr priests like Fr Jerzy Popieluszko and Fr Maximilian Kolbe. We've had great missionary priests like Fr Jacques Loew, of the worker priest movement, and Fr Charles de Foucauld. We even have great scientist priests like Fr Pierre Teilhard de Chardin, and Fr George Lemaître, the Father of the Big Bang theory of the creation of the universe. But despite this, we keep returning to this enigmatic 19th century French village priest. Why does St John Vianney still have such a hold over our imaginations?

The aftershocks of the *Curé d'Ars*

One of the reasons is we are still feeling the after-shocks of this priest's ministry 150 years after his death. When his bishop sent Jean Vianney to the remote, insignificant parish of Ars, 20 miles north of Lyons, he warned, "There is not much love of God in that parish; you will have to put some there." When he first arrived at Ars, his parish numbered only 230 people. At the height of his ministry, 300 people visited him everyday from all over France and even from foreign countries. In 1858, 80,000 pilgrims came to see him. Remember this was before motor ways, planes and high speed trains. It would have been quite an arduous journey to travel to this remote region of rural France. He was so popular a special coach service was put on to bring pilgrims from Lyon to Ars.

Why did the Curé d'Ars have this effect on people? I believe it was due to the fact that he had a keen sense of the need for salvation which he communicated with his whole being as a priest, particularly the 12 hour stints he served in the Confessional.

The secret of the *Curé d'Ars* success

We don't hear this word so often nowadays - Salvation. It's fallen out of fashion. We've never been more aware of our neuroses, phobias, anxieties, and syndromes. We've never had so many counsellors, psychologists, and life-style coaches. Never before have we been so knowledgeable about the weaknesses, frailties and illnesses of being human, but the need for salvation has fallen off most people's radars!

If people don't think they need saving, is it any wonder that they feel they have no need for a saviour! What is Salvation? The *Catechism* puts it succinctly: 'Called to beatitude but wounded by sin, man stands in need of salvation from God. Divine help comes to him in Christ through the law that guides him and the grace that sustains him.' (*CCC*, 1949).

This short quote puts its finger on what *Gaudium et Spes* describes as the fundamental split within man from which we need saving - we are called to beatitude but are wounded by sin. 'The call to grandeur and the depths of misery' (GS, 13). *Gaudium et Spes* goes on to explain our existential need for salvation, which we all experience even if we are reluctant or ignorant enough not to give it its proper name:

'Therefore man is split within himself. As a result, all of human life, whether individual or collective, shows itself to be a dramatic struggle between good and evil, between light and darkness. Indeed, man finds that by himself he is incapable of battling the assaults of evil successfully, so that everyone feels as though he is bound by chains. But the Lord Himself came to free and strengthen man, renewing him inwardly and casting out that "prince of this world" (*Jn* 12:31) who held him in the bondage of sin. For sin has diminished man, blocking his path to fulfilment.' (GS, 13).

This is the secret to St Jean Vianney's success and attraction as a priest - he had an acute sense of our call to grandeur and the depths of our misery. He saw his duty and role as a priest was to help each individual become aware of the drama of their split nature, and their need for divine help that only comes from Christ.

He saw this drama for what it clearly is - a life or death struggle - but at first he was surrounded by lapsed Catholics who did share the same sense of urgency. They were very similar to many of our own - the religiously indifferent and non-believing.

The description of our time that we find in the *General Directory for Catechesis* could have applied to people of his time in France: '...entire groups of the baptised have lost a living sense of the faith, or even no longer consider themselves members of the Church and live a life far removed from Christ and his Gospel... [they] live in a religious context in which Christian points of reference are perceived purely exteriorly.' (GDC, 58).

His response to this indifferentism was - "I weep because you do not weep". His pastoral priority was to teach his indifferent people to desire repentance and the beauty of God's forgiveness. He didn't court popularity, he didn't engage in person-centred, non-judgemental, positive regard, instead he was afire with the imperative that each person is struggling with a fundamental split in their nature

- called to beatitude but wounded by sin. This is how Pope John Paul II describes St Jean Vianney's pastoral strategy:

'He had the courage to denounce evil in all its forms; he did not keep silent, for it was a question of the eternal salvation of his faithful people: "If a pastor remains silent when he sees God insulted and souls going astray, woe to him! If he does not want to be damned, and if there is some disorder in his parish, he must trample upon human respect and the fear of being despised or hated"… But as a rule, he preferred to show the attractive side of virtue rather than the ugliness of vice, and if he spoke - sometimes in tears - about sin and the danger for salvation, he insisted on the tenderness of God who has been offended, and the happiness of being loved by God, united to God, living in his presence and for him.' (*Pope John Paul II, Maundy Thursday 1986*).

Questions for personal reflection

By way of conclusion, there follow some pertinent questions for your personal reflection:

Do I have the courage to confront evil in all its forms among my people and fellow clergy? - consumerism, hedonism, utilitarianism? - contraception, sterilisation, abortion? - alcoholism, addiction, pornography?

If I feel uncomfortable or conflicted about confronting evil in all its forms among my people and fellow clergy what does this say about me as a priest? Why don't I share St Jean Vianney's sense of the life or death struggle?

Do I desire true repentance? Do I teach my people the desire for true repentance? Or do I mostly focus of the beauty of God's forgiveness, brushing over the need for repentance and real change?

Do I live a life seeking to share in the virtues of Christ? Or do I automatically dismiss this as a counsel of idealistic perfection? When did I last preach about the attractiveness of a virtuous life?

Is it possible to talk to young people about salvation today? And is it necessary to go to confession regularly? What do you think the *Curé d'Ars* would say?

To conclude, let us consider to these words of the *Curé d'Ars*: 'Without the priest the death and passion of our Lord would be no use; the priest has the key of the heavenly treasures; he is God's steward and the administrator of his goods.'

'At the consecration the priest does not say, "This is the Body of our Lord". He says, "This is my Body". Behold the power of the priest! The tongue of the priest makes God from a morsel of bread! It is more than creating the world. "Marvellous dignity of priests!" exclaims St Augustine, "in their hands as in the womb of the blessed Virgin Mary, the Son of God becomes incarnate."'

A priest's share in the self-emptying of Christ

When Pope Benedict announced the special Year for Priests, he sought to draw our attention to the one characteristic essential to the identity of the priest - 'the priest's sacramental configuration to Christ the Head.' He went on to highlight the unique role the priest plays in the Church as representing Christ the Head: 'The centrality of Christ leads to a correct valuation of priestly ministry, without which there would be no Eucharist, no mission, not even the Church'. (*Letter Proclaiming a Year for Priests*)

What does it actually mean in practice for the priest to re-present, to make present Christ as Head of the Church? How can sinful, limited, weak men represent the headship of Christ, the second Person of the Holy Trinity, True God and true man, like us in all things except sin? In what way does our reception of the sacrament of Holy Orders make us different from lay men and women? How do we represent Christ the Head without slipping into a clericalism that isolates us from the laity, and traps us in a self-righteous, self-important caste? Alternatively, in an age of false egalitarianism how do we convince others of our priestly vocation to be pastors and leaders of our communities?

Pope John Paul II's love for the Curé D'Ars

To begin to answer some of these fundamental questions I
have turned to Pope John Paul II, a saint in the making,
and someone who had an acute sense of the importance
of priests to the life and mission of the Church. Every
Maundy Thursday Pope John Paul II addressed a homily
to the priests of the world to encourage and educate us
about the dignity and responsibility of being priests.

Undergoing his seminary training in secret during the
brutal Nazi occupation of Poland, hiding from the Gestapo
and SS who were hunting down seminarians, Karol
Wojtyla came to Ars in 1947, less than one year after his
ordination. This is what he tells us about the impact of his
visit to Ars on his understanding of the priesthood:

'With great emotion I visited the little church where St
John Vianney heard confessions, taught catechism, and
gave his homilies. It was an unforgettable experience for
me...St John Vianney astonishes us because in him we
can see the power of grace working through human
limitations. It was his heroic service in the confessional
which particularly struck me.

'That humble priest, who would hear confessions more
than ten hours a day, eating little and sleeping only a few
hours, was able, at a difficult moment in history, to
inspire a kind of spiritual revolution in France, and not
only there. Thousands of people passed through Ars and

knelt at his confessional. Against the background of attacks on the Church and the clergy in the 19th century, his witness was truly revolutionary.

'My encounter with this saintly figure confirmed me in the conviction that a priest fulfils an essential part of his mission through the confessional - by voluntarily "making himself a prisoner of the confessional." (*Pope John Paul II*, *Gift and Mystery*, p57-58).

Pope John Paul makes two points that give us our compass bearings to begin to approach the question of how priests represent Christ the Head in the Church - the power of grace working through human limitations and total commitment to the confessional.

The power of grace working through human limitations

Let us never forget that being a priest is always a work of grace, and not something we have achieved through our own merits, natural abilities or academic achievements. Every time we look in the mirror and see the stole, chasuble or clerical collar we should feel a sense of humility, and to be honest, fear and trembling, about being priests.

When I read this passage from the *Decree on the Ministry and Life of Priests* I feel both humility and fear and trembling: 'Since every priest in his own way assumes the person of Christ he is endowed with a special grace. By this grace the priest, through his service of the people committed to his care and all the People of God, is able the better to pursue the perfection of Christ, whose place he takes.' (*Presbyterorum Ordinis*, 12).

Each one of us, in his own way, assumes the person of Christ through grace. We receive this grace to be able the better to pursue the perfection of Christ, whose place we take. This is wonderful and terrifying at the same time. We represent Christ the Head because through sacramental ordination we 'assume' the person of Christ, and, in our communities, through grace, we take the place of Christ, not just when we say the words of consecration during the Eucharist, but all the time, in every encounter.

Is this hopelessly idealistic? Is this placing an unrealistic burden of moral perfection on frail human beings? Yes, if we think this is something to achieve by force of will and strength of character, but no, not at all, if we see it as living lives that enable the power of grace to work through human limitations. The one thing necessary is for us to willingly seek to pursue the perfection of Christ, to seek to give nothing less than everything to being priests.

Pope Benedict has revealed that his intention in holding a special Year for Priests between 2009-2010 is principally to encourage priests to pursue the perfection of Christ, which he describes as follows, 'that indispensable struggle for moral perfection which must dwell in every truly priestly heart.' How can our people embrace the discipline and commitment necessary to become a holy people if we priests have forgotten, or dismissed as unrealistic, this 'indispensable struggle for moral perfection'? Geoffrey Chaucer had a pithy, down to earth saying, 'If gold rusts, what will iron do!' Well, through ordination we received the pure gold of grace to assume the person of Christ, to become *alter Christus* in our parish communities.

The following are hard questions to consider, but I feel we must look at them because when we presented ourselves for ordination we accepted the responsibility of leadership: Have so many Catholics become lapsed or lukewarm because they couldn't see Christ in us? Do people not see Christ in us because we've given up on the idea of being saints?

To be honest, I feel we must answer, 'Yes' to both questions. In many cases we behave no differently than other people, and sometimes it shames me to say, we behave towards each other in ways that are more cynical and cruel than other people outside the Church.

Total commitment to the confessional

Another excerpt from *Presbyterorum Ordinis* states, 'Priests will acquire holiness in their own distinctive way by exercising their functions sincerely and tirelessly in the Spirit of Christ.' (PO, 13). One of the unique ways we assume the person of Christ and stand in His place is through administering the sacraments. It is at the altar and in the confessional that we acquire holiness that is 'distinctive' to the priesthood, when we exercise these functions 'sincerely and tirelessly in the Spirit of Christ'.

Without in any way wanting to diminish the importance of the celebration of the Mass in the life of the priest, I believe it is necessary to address an imbalance that has crept into our ministry. With the decline in the faithful seeking forgiveness of their sins through the sacrament of reconciliation, for many priests the ministry of the confessional has also declined in importance and significance in their lives. It comes a poor second or third after the celebration of the Mass, and baptism. But this demotion of the sacrament of forgiveness in the life of the priest and his people cannot stand because it is a denial of the very heart of salvation.

I want to propose to you that the first step we need to take in promoting the need for frequent confession among our people is to first understand its significance in the life of the priest. Our starting point in re-discovering this significance is found in St Paul's letter to the Philippians: 'Let the same mind be in you that was in Christ Jesus, who, though he was in the form of God, did not regard equality with God as something to be exploited, but emptied himself, taking the form of a slave, being born in human likeness. And being found in human form, he humbled himself and became obedient to the point of death - even death on a cross.' (*Ph* 2:5-8). Every time we enter the confessional 'sincerely and tirelessly in the Spirit of Christ' we have the privilege and responsibility of participating in the self-emptying love, the kenosis of the Second Person of the Holy Trinity.

Why do I say this? When we sit down in the confessional and put on the purple stole and immerse ourselves - with compassion and understanding - in the banality of evil we are standing in the place of Christ in his self-emptying, redemptive love of sinners. In the confessional the priest enters the great mystery of the sinless God becoming sin out of redemptive love for humanity, as St Paul puts it in that profoundly mysterious sentence from II Corinthians: 'For our sake he made him to be sin who knew no sin, so that in him we might become the righteousness of God.' (2 *Co* 5:21).

The 'stripping' of Christ

I am convinced that if we, as priests, want to seek the moral perfection of Christ and sincerely and tirelessly exercise our functions in the Spirit of Christ we must begin here in the self-emptying of Christ in the confessional. Out of love for mankind the Son of God stripped himself of his divine glory when he left heaven and became a man, and throughout his life on earth he allowed himself to be stripped of his dignity as God and as man. These indignities and humiliations were not accidental or expected but accepted by God to teach us so many things:

The 'stripping' of Bethlehem

The Son of God was born into the abject poverty of the stable, his crib - a food trough for animals. As St Francis puts it, 'O marvellous humility, O astonishing poverty! The King of angels, the Lord of heaven and earth, is laid in a manger'.

The 'stripping' of the Presentation

The Son of God is presented for purification at the Temple by his mother, according to the Law, as if they were sinners in need of sacrificial purification, when in fact both were sinless. As St John Baptist de la Salle's puts it, 'Is there anything that could be more humiliating for the Son of God than to appear as a sinner, although He was holiness itself'.

The 'stripping' of Baptism

The Son of God associates and identifies with sinners by receiving baptism from John, though He does not need to repent, for He has committed no sin. As Blessed Columba Marmion puts it, 'He who thus proclaims Himself a sinner is the Second Person of the Holy Trinity, before whom the angels veil their faces, singing, 'Holy, holy, holy.'

The 'stripping' of the Eucharist

The Gospel of John gives an account of Jesus stripping Himself to wash the apostles' feet. St John sets Jesus' stripping in the context of the over-arching self-emptying of the incarnation: 'Jesus, knowing that the Father had given all things into his hands, and that he had come from God and was going to God, got up from the table, took off his outer robe, and tied a towel around himself.' (*Jn* 13:3-4). Jesus accepts this humiliation, as He has done throughout his life, to communicate and make real His divine, unconditional, self-giving love, even to the point of a humiliating death.

The 'stripping' of the Cross

Jesus' death on the Cross was foreshadowed by all the previous 'strippings' of his life. As Gerald O'Collins so expressively conveys 'God is not only absolutely self-fulfilled, but also absolutely self-giving. Precisely because he was divine, Jesus gave himself away.' (*Christology*, p226-227).

Sharing the self-emptying of Christ

What does this reflection on the 'stripping' of Christ tell us about how, as priests, we represent Christ the Head? What are the hallmarks of Christ's self-emptying? He freely gives himself away to save us from our sins. He does this through a vulnerability that is dignified, a humility that leads, a weakness that transforms.

What does this mean for us? We must not hide behind our clerical collars. What I mean by this is we must not assume a clerical *persona* to protect our real selves from our people. We must always be ourselves, not some 'priestly' caricature. It is only if others feel they are in contact with a real person that they will begin to 'really' hear the Gospel.

Giving nothing less than everything

Naturally, many priests will find it threatening to accept the vulnerability, honesty and self-emptying of Jesus, concerned that they would be totally 'consumed' by their people. I have two reflections on this: first, Jesus gives Himself away out of love of others, and becomes more Himself, proving the truth of his teaching, '*He who would find his life must lose his life*'. (*Lk* 9:24; cf. *Mt* 10:39). Second, to be able to give himself away, Jesus had to retire to lonely places to rest and pray to the Father.

Celibacy and obedience

There is nothing more counter-cultural than our priestly vows of celibacy and obedience. To 'outsiders' these are seen as the epitome of unnatural restrictions of freedom of choice and human rights. But seen from the 'inside' of Revelation in Scripture and Tradition, celibacy and obedience are gifts that enable the priest to make present the truth of Christ's love emptied out in service of the Church, the people of God.

Through the daily gift of our bodies and the daily gift of our wills we consciously seek the perfection of Christ. In the Latin rite, celibacy and obedience are the indispensable conditions that enable us to stand in the place of Christ, representing His total, self-giving love.

Servant leadership

Seen in the context of the series of 'strippings' that characterise Jesus' life and ministry it doesn't come as a surprise that he exhorts the apostles to a revolutionary style of leadership of the Church: 'But Jesus called them to him and said, "You know that the rulers of the Gentiles lord it over them, and their great ones are tyrants over them. It will not be so among you; but whoever wishes to be great among you must be your servant, and whoever wishes to be first among you must be your slave; just as the Son of Man came not to be served but to serve, and to give his life a ransom for many."' (*Mt* 20: 25-28).

There is a danger with the 'servant leader' model. It can be erroneously understood as meaning that as priests we only give the people what they want, and make no demands of them. That we are merely the servants of their needs as they understand or want them. For example, that we provide the sacraments on demand irrespective of their lack of faith or practise, or not challenging the wide-spread and pernicious belief among Catholics that they can personally choose what it means to be Catholic, even if their beliefs and behaviours contradict the doctrine and morals of the Church.

Jesus exhorts the apostles, and priests, to be servants like him, who was a servant of God and a servant of people's true needs. Therefore, a true servant leader after the Spirit of Christ will challenge, correct and encourage his people to be authentic Catholics. As it puts it in the *Decree on the Ministry and Life of Priests*:

'They should act towards people not according to what may please people, but according to the demands of Christian doctrine and life. They should teach them and warn them as their dearest children, according to the words of the apostle: "be urgent in season and out of season, convince, rebuke, and exhort, be unfailing in patience and in teaching"' (2 *Tm* 4:2). (PO, 6).

To act towards people not according to what may please them but according to the demands of doctrine is a daunting challenge, and maybe one many of us, including bishops, have shirked because nobody wants to be unpopular and ridiculed. But this is the 'stripping' that is demanded by the times in which we live:

- We must tell the truth that Jesus is the only Saviour of the world.

- We must tell the truth that the fullness of saving truth is only to be found in the Catholic Church.
- We must tell the truth about contraception and IVF.
- We must tell the truth about consumerism and wealth.
- We must tell the truth about homosexuality, pre-marital sex and adultery.
- We must tell the truth about the authoritarianism of the liberal establishment.
- We must tell the truth about abortion and so-called 'safe sex'.

We do this not in a spirit of adversity or condemnation, but as a service of love, because countless numbers of people are being harmed by the lies that are masquerading as truth in our society. Souls are being put in mortal danger, and we must strip off our outer-garments and wash the feet of suffering humanity. In the light of the above, I would encourage you to reflect on this passage from John's Gospel:

'Jesus, knowing that the Father had given all things into his hands, and that he had come from God and was going to God, got up from the table, took off his outer robe, and tied a towel around himself. Then he poured water into a basin and began to wash the disciples' feet and to wipe them with the towel that was tied around him. 'He came to Simon Peter, who said to him, "Lord, are you going to wash my feet?" Jesus answered, "You do not know now what I am doing, but later you will understand". Peter said to him, "You will never wash my feet." Jesus answered, "Unless I wash you, you have no share with me". 'Simon Peter said to him, "Lord, not my feet only but also my hands and my head!" Jesus said to him, "One who has bathed does not need to wash, except for the feet, but is entirely clean. And you are clean, though not all of you." For he knew who was to betray him; for this reason he said, "Not all of you are clean." 'After he had washed their feet, had put on his robe, and had returned to the table, he said to them, "Do you know what I have done to you? You call me Teacher and Lord — and you are right, for that is what I am. So if I, your Lord and Teacher, have washed your feet, you also ought to wash one another's feet. For I have set you an example, that you also should do as I have done to you. Very truly, I tell you, servants are not greater than their master, nor are messengers greater than the one who sent them. If you know these things, you are blessed if you do them.' (*Jn* 13:3-17).

A priest's freedom for mission

Pope Benedict made his announcement of the special Year for Priests at a plenary assembly of the Congregation for the Clergy on the theme of 'The missionary identity of priests in the Church as an intrinsic dimension of the exercise of the *'tre munera'*.' He makes it clear that developing the missionary role of the priest is the fundamental purpose of this special year. As Pope Benedict puts it:

'The missionary dimension of the priest is born from his sacramental configuration to Christ the Head... It also seems urgent to recover that consciousness that drives priests to be present, identifiable and recognisable both by the judgment of faith, or by personal virtues, or also by their dress, in the realms of culture and charity, ever at the heart of the mission of the Church.' (*Letter Proclaiming a Year for Priests*)

St John Vianney - model of the missionary priest

St Jean Vianney was a missionary priest who was acutely conscious of the need to be present, identifiable and recognisable in the spheres of culture and charity in the parish of Ars. Jean Vianney's appointment to the village of Ars in the 19th century has been described as being the

clerical equivalent of being sent to Siberia. The Vicar
General told him that 'There is not much love in that
parish - you will instil some into it'.

When he arrived in the village he found an
exceedingly dilapidated church and a wretched
presbytery. The village had been without its own priest
for years, and the practice of the Faith had declined to a
devout minority. As with the rest of rural France, the
observance of Sunday as a holy day had collapsed, with
villagers working in the fields in the morning and Sunday
afternoon and evening was spent in binge drinking in the
many taverns. (cf. Dom Ernest Grof, *The Curé d'Ars*)

The missionary situation that Jean Vianney faced -
religious indifference, ignorance about the Faith, and a
collapse of practice - had been created by the legally-
enforced secularisation of the French Revolution, which
for a period banned the Catholic Church, and drove
Catholic priests underground under threat of death.

In order to bring the love of Christ to his loveless village
the Curé d'Ars employed a missionary strategy. He visited
every household in the parish, and walked the fields - breviary
in hand - to speak to the peasants about their concerns. He
also lived the life-style of the peasants, eating the same
type of restricted diet, sometimes even worse as a penance.

He was known among his people as a man of intense
prayer and self-denial. Sometimes he spent 7 hours a day
writing his homilies, which was the main way he catechised

his people. He also repaired and enriched the parish church with his own money, employing the best goldsmiths and embroiderers of Lyons to restore the house of God.

One of his most ambitious projects was to open a free boarding school and day school for destitute children that he called 'Providence'. He was responsible for providing the children with food and clothing. His 'Providence' school became the inspiration for similar schools throughout France. He had daily contact with the children, teaching them the Catechism and eating his meals with them and the staff. As we can see, St Jean Vianney had a holistic 'incarnational' understanding of mission, responding to both the spiritual and material needs of his people. Obviously mission was central to his self-understanding and role as a priest. What role does evangelisation and mission play in the Church in England and Wales, and in our lives as priests?

Fit for Mission?

When I was Bishop of Lancaster, my then diocese was involved in the *Fit for Mission?* renewal initiative. As part of this 2-year programme all 108 parishes completed a parish evaluation form that looked at the sacramental and mission life of each parish.

The passage of Scripture that guided our mission review was: 'Then Jesus called the twelve together and gave them power and authority…and he sent them out to

proclaim the kingdom of God and to heal.' (*Lk* 9:1-2).
Our survey revealed that most of our parishes were good
at being gathered by the Lord, with a focus on liturgy and
sacramental provision, but the whole dimension of being
sent out in mission was undeveloped or inactive.

As a Church we have become, for the most part, very
inward looking and self involved. The reasons for this are
complex, but I would like to propose that the fundamental
reason is that we do not see mission as important or
central to our identity as Catholics as participating in the
Mass or sacramental life. There is a short circuit in our
Christian discipleship in that we have forgotten that Jesus
gathers us together through the sacraments to give us
power and authority so that we go out into the world to
proclaim the kingdom and to heal.

How do we rectify this short circuit in our life as
Catholics? We need to begin to see that mission is not
optional or peripheral to our lives but is fundamental and
necessary in our relationship with God, as fundamental
and necessary as prayer and the Mass.

Mission has its source in the Holy Trinity

I believe that if we start seeing mission as a fundamental
aspect of the inner life of the Holy Trinity we will re-evaluate
the importance of mission in our own lives. The Holy Trinity
is foundational to all Christian teaching and understanding
and is the source of all the other mysteries of faith. The

Second Vatican Council's Decree on the Missionary Activity of the Church (*Ad Gentes*) begins by setting the Church's mission in the context of the mission of the Holy Trinity:

'The pilgrim Church is missionary by her very nature, since it is from the mission of the Son and the mission of the Holy Spirit that she draws her origin, in accordance with the decree of God the Father. This decree, however, flows from the "ever upwelling love" or charity of God the Father who, being the "principle without principle" from whom the Son is begotten and the Holy Spirit proceeds through the Son, freely creating us on account of His surpassing and merciful kindness and graciously calling us moreover to share with Him His life and His glory, has generously poured out, and does not cease to pour out still, His divine goodness.' (*Ad Gentes*, 3)

What does 'mission' mean? Mission means to be sent. Remembering back to our Latin, I'm sure we all recollect that it comes from the word *missio* meaning 'to send'. Our lives as Christians are caught up in a series of 'sendings', a series of 'missions':

The 'sending' of the Trinity

The divine mission of the Trinity is the most fundamental, most profound mission that energises and directs all the other 'missions'. The sending of the second and third Persons of the Trinity by the Father in eternity and time is the basic mystery of God going out, reaching out in love. As St Augustine expresses it, 'The Father is the Lover, the Son the Beloved and the Holy Spirit the mutual love that passes between Father and Son.'

The 'sending' of the Son

Over and over again the New Testament describes the incarnation in terms of the Father sending the Son. Jesus describes himself as one sent on a mission on behalf of his Father: 'Jesus said to them again, "Peace be with you. As the Father has sent me, so I send you."' (*Jn* 20:21). 'As you have sent me into the world, so I have sent them into the world.' (*Jn* 17:18). 'But when the fullness of time had come, God sent his Son, born of a woman, born under the law, in order to redeem those who were under the law, so that we might receive adoption as children. And because you are children, God has sent the Spirit of his Son into our hearts, crying, "Abba! Father!"' (*Ga* 4:4-6).

The 'sending' of the Holy Spirit

The Church as an institution and communion exists because of the 'sending' of the Holy Spirit by the Father and the Son. If it wasn't for this 'sending' we would not be here today as priests of the Catholic Church reflecting on the future of the Church in the light of the charism - the gift of the Holy Spirit - of St Jean Vianney.

Everything that makes up our identity and role, that gives our lives meaning, is due to the ceaseless sending of

the Holy Spirit. Our 'being' is shaped by the mission of
the Holy Spirit: 'But the Advocate, the Holy Spirit, whom
the Father will send in my name, will teach you
everything, and remind you of all that I have said to you.'
(*Jn* 14:26). As Pope John Paul II puts it, the Holy Spirit
remains the transcendent and principal agent for the
accomplishment of Christ's mission in the human spirit
and in the history of the world. (*Redemptoris missio*, 21).

The 'sending' of the Apostles

Even before Ascension and Pentecost the Lord sent the
apostles out to proclaim the Gospel. 'Apostle' means
'somebody sent' which reveals to us that Jesus chose
twelve men for the express purpose of sending them out
into the world. As St Mark expresses it, 'the Lord Jesus
called to Himself those whom He wished; and He caused
twelve of them to be with Him, and to be sent out
preaching'. (*Mk* 3:13; cf. *Mt* 10:1-42).

It is clear that Jesus saw the 'sending' of the apostles
as being identified with, and a continuation, of His
'sending' by the Father: 'Jesus said to them again, "Peace
be with you. As the Father has sent me, so I send you."
When he had said this, he breathed on them and said to
them, "Receive the Holy Spirit. If you forgive the sins of
any, they are forgiven them; if you retain the sins of any,
they are retained."' (*Jn* 20:21-23).

The 'sending' of the Church

The missionary imperative that Jesus clearly imparted to the Church is not the expansion of a social, political or economic organisation but a divine imperative that has its origin, its dynamic impetus, from the inner life and love of the Holy Trinity.

The missionary mandate of Jesus to the Church derives from the processions of Persons in the Trinity and the missions of the divine Persons, the Incarnation and the descent of the Holy Spirit: "Go, therefore, and make disciples of all nations, baptising them in the name of the Father and of the Son and of the Holy Spirit; teaching them to observe all that I have commanded you". (*Mt* 28:19). Therefore, the mission of the Church is a profoundly holy and sacred activity, that should be a source of prayer, spirituality and commitment equal to the Eucharist in the life of the Church.

The 'sending' of today's priests

I think we would all agree that we owe the Missionary Orders our respect and support for their dedication to evangelisation and catechesis around the world. However, I am convinced that this division between missionary and secular priests has led us, the secular priests, to mistakenly think that mission is not necessarily central to our identity and role.

Mission is not the sole preserve of missionary order priests, but the truth of the matter is that we are all missionary priests. This is what Pope John Paul II says about the priest as missionary: 'As co-workers of the bishops, priests are called by virtue of the sacrament of Orders to share in concern for the Church's mission: "The spiritual gift that priests have received in ordination prepares them, not for any narrow and limited mission, but for the most universal and all embracing mission of salvation 'to the end of the earth.' For every priestly ministry shares in the universal scope of the mission that Christ entrusted to his apostles." All priests must have the mind and the heart of missionaries…' (Pope John Paul II, *Redemptoris missio*, 67).

Reason why we're not missionary

There are many reasons why we hold back from our vocation to be missionary priests. To start with, let's be honest, mission is not a priority among most of the bishops. In this age of ecumenism and inter-faith dialogue most of us have lost our confidence in the uniqueness and irreplaceable value of the Catholic Faith. For many it has become embarrassing and unacceptable to say that Jesus is the only Saviour of mankind, that salvation does not exist apart from Jesus Christ, and that the Church 'subsists' in the Catholic Church, and nowhere else.

Secondly, we are faced with a post-Christian, secular society that in its ignorance thinks it knows what Christianity is, and aggressively projects and attacks the caricature of the Catholic Faith that it holds as being the truth. Much of the media, political parties and education establishment don't want to engage in a real dialogue with us because they much prefer the 'caricature'. This is always the way when an ideology takes hold of a culture, propaganda replaces truth, and half-truths and untruths are repeated often enough to become firmly lodged in the public consciousness as being The Truth. What St Paul wrote to Timothy applies to us even more: 'For the time is coming when people will not put up with sound doctrine, but having itching ears, they will accumulate for themselves teachers to suit their own desires, and will turn away from listening to the truth and wander away to myths.' (2 *Tm* 4:3-4).

It is a sad truth that many people are so alienated from the Church, the language of the Bible, and their need for salvation, that they are either indifferent or violently allergic to Christianity. Also, it is heart-breaking to admit that the behaviour of some Catholics, such as paedophile priests and the failure of some in authority in the Church, has damaged the credibility of the Church.

How to be missionary today

I am convinced that in order to evangelise this generation we must follow the advice of Newman and de Foucauld and concentrate our missionary efforts on showing the unconditional love of Christ for suffering humanity though practical acts of justice, social care and peace. In particular, we must act in solidarity with the poor and all those on the margins of society, migrants, drug addicts, alcoholics, men and women in the sex industry, those suffering mental illness.

We must do this without any ulterior motives, such as seeking converts. We must only undertake this work to show them the love of Jesus Christ. It is only when or if they ask us why we do this work that we can gently begin to talk to them about Jesus, and only at the pace that they want. If they reject Jesus, but accept His practical love through our actions, we must be content with that.

By way of conclusion let us consider two sayings that indicate the direction we must take to face the missionary challenge that faces us - from Blessed Cardinal Newman and Blessed Charles de Foucauld:

'That we preach Jesus without preaching, not by words but by our example, by the catching force, the sympathetic influence of what we do, the evident fullness of love our hearts bear to You, Lord'. (*Cardinal Newman*)

'That we learn that it is possible to do good to men without using words, without preaching, without fuss, but by silence, devotion, poverty, humility and obscurity.' (*Blessed de Foucauld*).

A priest's immersion in the truth of Faith

Let us turn our attention to the spirituality of priests, which brings us to the theme of these reflections, 'Rich in Christ, rich in love'.

Over forty years a priest I am certain that in order for you to be effective and fulfilled in your ministry, you must be immersed in Jesus Christ. You must eat, drink, sleep, think, and breathe Jesus Christ. Only in this way will you be rich in love - love of God, love of others - your brother priests, bishop, pope and people - and, just as importantly, love of yourself. When we are rich in the love of Christ, it both heals and challenges us and all others with whom we come into contact.

A poverty of love

But the tragedy is when - as priests - we are poor in Christ, because then we are poor in love. We all know the signs of this poverty of love in the priesthood:

- The bitterness and weary disillusionment that has become all too common.
- The passive aggression that so easily erupts into hostility towards brother priests, bishops, and the Holy Father.

- The prevalence of addictive escapism through alcoholism, internet pornography, etc.
- The obsession with the 'glittering prizes' of clerical status and power in the Church.
- The rejection of the authority of doctrine and the hierarchy, with priests thinking and behaving as if they had autonomous power unto themselves.

To counter this poverty of Christ and poverty of love, the first thing we have to do is realise that as priests we have a special vocation and opportunity to become rich in Christ because we have emptied ourselves of everything the world values - sexual love, children and wealth - in order to be filled by Christ. This is the meaning of being *in persona Christi*. As we examined earlier, through ordination we have been endowed with a special grace to 'assume the person of Christ', to stand in the place of Christ. This special grace enables and empowers us to be 'stripped' and 'sent' as Christ before us.

The need for a new spirituality

How do we become rich in Christ? This is a question of developing a spirituality for priests and people that meets the needs of today. Every age of the Church has seen the emergence of spiritualities and devotions that meet the existential and social needs of the times. For example, among the many Catholic spiritualities:

Desert Father spirituality emphasised spiritual combat and single-minded seeking of God in reaction to the complexity and compromise of State and Church relations.

Franciscan spirituality emphasised the imitation of the poverty and simplicity of the Gospel in reaction to the growing wealth and power the State and Church.

Devotion to the Sacred Heart of Jesus emphasised the merciful love and divine humanity of Jesus in reaction to the strictures of Jansenism.

I would like to propose to you that during a time when relativism and utilitarianism is in the ascendancy in our society, a time that is so obviously confused about the truth and the possibility of there being truth, we need a spirituality that has the Truth of Faith at its heart. During his pontificate Pope Benedict is continuing to develop a spirituality of the Truth, which he is inviting priests to join him in living and promoting among their people. During the Chrism Mass at St Peter's in 2008 the Holy Father makes clear the link between holiness and the Truth:

'On the eve of my priestly ordination, fifty-eight years ago, I opened the Sacred Scripture, because I wanted to receive once more a word from the Lord for that day and for my future journey as a priest. My gaze fell on this passage: "Sanctify them in the truth; your word is truth". Then I realised: the Lord is speaking about me, and he is speaking to me. This very same thing will be accomplished tomorrow in me. When all is said and done, we are not consecrated by rites, even though rites are necessary. The bath in which the Lord immerses us is himself - the Truth in person. Priestly ordination means: being immersed in him, immersed in the Truth. I belong in a new way to him and thus to others, "that his Kingdom may come". Dear friends, in this hour of the renewal of promises, we want to pray to the Lord to make us men of truth, men of love, men of God. Let us implore him to draw us ever anew into himself, so that we may become truly priests of the New Covenant. Amen.'

A spirituality of Truth

'Sanctify them in the truth; your word is truth'. (*Jn* 17:17). Let us look more closely at the meaning of sanctification and truth.

Sanctification

The search for, and gift of, holiness is the impetus, the driver of every true spirituality. What does this mean? That spirituality is man's response to God's initiative that seeks to introduce us into the intimacy of Trinitarian life. At the heart of spirituality is sanctifying grace. This is how the *Catechism* defines sanctifying grace: 'Sanctifying grace is the gratuitous gift of his life that God makes to us; it is infused by the Holy Spirit into the soul to heal it of sin and to sanctify it. Sanctifying grace makes us "pleasing to God".' (*CCC*, 2023-2024). In

Romans, St Paul describes sanctification as being *'conformed to the image of God's Son'* (*Rm* 8:28-30).

Truth

One of the hallmarks of Pope Benedict's theology and spirituality is his understanding that ultimate truth is a person - Jesus Christ. As he explained to young people in New York in 2008:

'Dear friends, truth is not an imposition. Nor is it simply a set of rules. It is a discovery of the One who never fails us; the One whom we can always trust. In seeking truth we come to live by belief because ultimately truth is a person: Jesus Christ. That is why authentic freedom is not an opting out. It is an opting in; nothing less than letting go of self and allowing oneself to be drawn into Christ's very being for others.'

As was mentioned earlier, we must eat, drink, sleep, think, and breathe Jesus Christ or as Pope Benedict puts it we must be sanctified in the Truth, we must immerse ourselves in the Truth of Jesus Christ.

We must immerse ourselves in the Scriptural Truth of Jesus

How many times have we heard this as priests that it passes over us like water off a duck's back? Does Scripture remain a closed book to us, not really touching our lives deep down, where we really live? Would we

52

rather do anything thing else but sit down in a quiet room and open a Bible? Pope Benedict expresses it very well when he asks:

'Are we deeply engaged with this word to the point that it really leaves a mark on our lives and shapes our thinking? Or is it rather the case that our thinking is constantly being shaped by all the things that others say and do? Aren't prevailing opinions the criterion by which we all too often measure ourselves? Do we not perhaps remain, when all is said and done, mired in the superficiality in which people today are generally caught up? Do we allow ourselves truly to be deeply purified by the word of God?' (*Letter Proclaiming a Year for Priests*)

We must immerse ourselves in the Doctrinal Truth of Jesus

How many of us have a copy of the *Catechism of the Catholic Church* that is as pristine and unused as the day we bought it and put in on our bookshelf? There is a common mistaken attitude among some priests and laity who have had some kind of theological education that they are at a level beyond the *Catechism*. It's as if many priests and catechists believe that somehow we have gone beyond the need for catechisms that we're too sophisticated and diverse to be bound by a simple exposition of the doctrine of the Church.

However, I believe that the use of the *Catechism* in our pastoral ministry is a good measure of our humility and obedience to the Truth. Pope John Paul II saw the *Catechism* as a fruit of the Second Vatican Council, and a gift of the Holy Spirit to the Church. I am convinced that the Holy Spirit has given us the *Catechism of the Catholic Church* at this time of dissent and apostasy to 'sanctify us in the Truth'. The four pillars of the *Catechism* - Profession of Faith, Celebration of the Sacraments, Moral life in Christ and Prayer - provide us with a sure foundation from which to challenge the ignorance and rejection of the truth that is so widespread in society and even in the Church.

The doctrinal picture of Jesus in the *Catechism* is the Jesus of history understood in greater depth through the Spirit inspired inter-play of Scripture, Tradition and the Magisterium. I suggest that each reader make the resolution to prayerfully read paragraphs 422-682 about Jesus Christ. Reading these paragraphs has been described as rediscovering, as if for the first time, how great the figure of Jesus is!

We must immerse ourselves in the Spiritual Truth of Jesus

It's a truism to say that a priest must be a man of prayer, but the reality of life as a priest living on his own in a presbytery is that the door bell and telephone so easily squeeze out time for personal prayer. And to be honest, for many of us dealing with the requests and demands of pastoral work can be easier than sitting in stillness and silence necessary for prayer. As a result of these pressures prayer can often be forced back into the obligations of the Divine Office and celebrating the Mass! However, we all know it's true that if we don't make time for personal prayer even praying the Office and Celebrating the Mass can remain on a surface-level and become just something we must do!

My recommendation is always make time every day to pray before the Blessed Sacrament. To truly re-present Christ at the altar we must make an altar of our heart. The heart in prayer is an altar on which the Holy Spirit places and engraves the eternal Gospel - Jesus. (Fr Jean Corbon). This work of engraving the altar of our heart can sometimes be ecstatic and profound, often it can be painful and mundane, but either way in time the Spirit sanctifies our innermost being.

Love of the truth does not come cheap

Pope Benedict expresses the importance of the priest's struggle for the Truth as follows:

'To be immersed in God's truth…also means to acknowledge that the truth makes demands, to stand up, in matters great and small, to the lie which in so many different ways is present in the world; accepting the struggles associated with the truth, because its inmost joy is present within us. Nor, when we talk about being sanctified in the truth, should we forget that in Jesus Christ truth and love are one. Being immersed in him means being immersed in his goodness, in true love. True love does not come cheap, it can also prove quite costly. It resists evil in order to bring men true good.' (*Pope Benedict XVI, Chrism Mass Homily, 2009*).

St Jean Vianney knew what it meant to be sanctified in the truth of Jesus Christ. He was a priest who lived his daily life immersed in the Truth of Jesus. Pope John Paul II notes that the Curé d'Ars had a particular devotion to praying before the Blessed Sacrament even in the midst of 300 people seeking him out every day and spending 12 hours in the Confessional!

He spent long hours before the tabernacle before daybreak or in the evening, depending on the demands of his pastoral work. Often during his homilies he would turn towards the tabernacle and say with deep emotion, 'He is there!' One of the consequences of his manifest devotion to prayer before the Blessed Sacrament was that his parishioners soon took up the habit of coming to pray before the Blessed Sacrament. Pope John Paul sums up the secret of St Jean Vianney's success as a priest immersed in Christ:

'Saint John Marie Vianney did not content himself with the ritual carrying out of the activities of his ministry. It was his heart and his life which he sought to conform to Christ. Prayer was the soul of his life: silent and contemplative prayer, generally in his church at the foot of the tabernacle.' (*Pope John Paul II, Maundy Thursday, 1986*).

A meditation with the Curé d'Ars

I would like to conclude with this passage from the *Catechism of the Catholic Church*, one of two that relates to the Curé of Ars. I invite you to read it slowly as a meditation.

'"Hope does not disappoint us, because God's love has been poured into our hearts by the Holy Spirit who has been given to us." Prayer, formed by the liturgical life, draws everything into the love by which we are loved in Christ and which enables us to respond to him by loving as he has loved us. Love is the source of prayer; whoever draws from it reaches the summit of prayer. In the words of the Curé of Ars:

"I love you, O my God, and my only desire is to love you until the last breath of my life. I love you, O my infinitely lovable God, and I would rather die loving you, than live without loving you. I love you, Lord, and the only grace I ask is to love you eternally. ...My God, if my tongue cannot say in every moment that I love you, I want my heart to repeat it to you as often as I draw breath".' (*CCC*, 2658).